I0814847

DISCOVERING THE UNITED STATES

Illinois

BY KELLY ANNE WHITE

Kids Core

An Imprint of Abdo Publishing
abdobooks.com

abdobooks.com

Published by Abdo Publishing, a division of ABDO, PO Box 398166, Minneapolis, Minnesota 55439.

Printed in China.
052024
092024

Cover Photo: Semmick Photo/Shutterstock Images
Interior Photos: Universal History Archive/Universal Images Group/Getty Images, 4–5; Chicago History Museum/Archive Photos/Getty Images, 7; Ken Schulze/Shutterstock Images, 8; Bonnie Taylor Barry/Shutterstock Images, 10 (top left); Shutterstock Images, 10 (top right), 10 (bottom left), 10 (bottom right), 14, 26, 28 (bottom left); New York Public Library/Smith Collection/Gado Images/Alamy, 12–13; Michael Hickey/Getty Images Sport/Getty Images, 17; Nam Y. Huh/AP Images, 18; Paul Brady Photography/Shutterstock Images, 20–21; Nicola Patterson/Shutterstock Images, 23, 28 (top right); Susan Montgomery/Shutterstock Images, 25; Red Line Editorial, 28 (top left), 29; Heather Raulerson/Shutterstock Images, 28 (bottom right)

Editor: Haley Williams
Series Design: Katharine Hale

Library of Congress Control Number: 2023949384

Publisher's Cataloging-in-Publication Data

Names: White, Kelly Anne, author.
Title: Illinois / by Kelly Anne White
Description: Minneapolis, Minnesota: Abdo Publishing, 2025 | Series: Discovering the United States | Includes online resources and index.
Identifiers: ISBN 9781098293833 (lib. bdg.) | ISBN 9798384913108 (ebook)
Subjects: LCSH: U.S. states--Juvenile literature. | Illinois--History--Juvenile literature. | Midwest States--Juvenile literature. | Physical geography--United States--Juvenile literature.
Classification: DDC 973--dc23

All population data taken from:
"Estimates of Population by Sex, Race, and Hispanic Origin: April 1, 2020 to July 1, 2022." *US Census Bureau, Population Division*, June 2023, census.gov.

CONTENTS

The site of the Chicago World's Fair was nicknamed the White City after the large, white buildings that were designed for the event.

CHAPTER 1

The Chicago World's Fair

It was May 1, 1893. The World's Columbian Exposition was starting in Illinois. This was also called the Chicago World's Fair. World's fairs are events where people from around the world can showcase new ideas, inventions, and technology.

The World's Columbian Exposition ran for almost six months. During that time, more than 27 million visitors came. People could see and ride the world's first Ferris wheel. They could taste new foods, such as Cracker Jack popcorn and brownies.

The fair also featured many new inventions, including the zipper and **automatic** dishwasher. Many of these inventions continue to be used today. The Chicago World's Fair is still considered an important event in both Illinois and US history.

Land and Climate

Illinois is located in the US Midwest region. It borders five states. Wisconsin is to the north.

The first Ferris wheel stood 264 feet (81 m) tall and cost $0.50 to ride.

Today, the Illinois government protects the small areas of prairie left in the state.

Indiana and Kentucky are to the east. To the west are Iowa and Missouri. Lake Michigan is on the northeast edge of Illinois. And the Mississippi River runs along its western border.

Illinois is a very flat state. Its nickname is the Prairie State. Illinois used to be covered in grasslands known as prairies. But over time, most of the prairies in Illinois were turned into farmland. Today, about 75 percent of the state's land is used for farming.

Prairie Wildlife

Illinois has a variety of wildlife in its prairies. Animals such as coyotes, foxes, and bobcats are known to live there. The prairies are also home to groundhogs, gophers, and badgers. Some prairie birds include meadowlarks and sparrows. The greater prairie chicken is an endangered bird in Illinois.

Illinois Facts

DATE OF STATEHOOD
December 3, 1818

CAPITAL
Springfield

POPULATION
12,582,032

AREA
57,914 square miles
(149,997 sq km)

STATE BIRD

Northern cardinal

STATE TREE

White oak

STATE FLOWER

Violet

STATE INSECT

Monarch butterfly

Each US state has a different population, size, and capital city. States also have state symbols.

There are also suburbs and cities in Illinois. Chicago is the largest city in the state. It is often called the Windy City. Chicago has 26 miles (42 km) of shoreline on Lake Michigan.

Illinois experiences all four seasons. Spring and fall are mild. Summers are hot and **humid**. The state also gets rain and storms in the summer. Winters in Illinois are often very cold. The state is known for getting a lot of snow. Northern Illinois winters can be very snowy, especially near Lake Michigan. Tornadoes are also common in Illinois. This is due to the state's flat landscape.

Further Evidence

Look at the website below. Does it give any new evidence to support Chapter One?

Illinois

abdocorelibrary.com/discovering-illinois

Chicago is located on the traditional homelands of the Ojibwe, Odawa, Potawatomi, and several other American Indian nations.

CHAPTER 2

The People of Illinois

The first people arrived in Illinois around 13,000 years ago. The state is named after a group of American Indian nations known as the Illiniwek, or Illinois. The Illiniwek were made up of several smaller tribes. These included the Cahokia, Peoria, and Kaskaskia.

The year 1818 on Illinois's state flag represents when Illinois became a state, and 1868 represents when the state seal was first used.

The first Europeans explored Illinois in 1673. Their names were Louis Jolliet and Jacques Marquette. During the mid-1700s, more European **settlers** arrived in the state.

In 1832, the US government forced the Illiniwek nations to leave their homeland. Today, the **descendants** of the Illiniwek live in Oklahoma. They are known as the Peoria Tribe of Indians.

In 2022, more than 12.5 million people lived in Illinois. About 60 percent of the population was white. Hispanic or Latino people made up about 18 percent. Around 15 percent of people were Black, and 6 percent were Asian.

Culture

Illinois has several **iconic** foods. The horseshoe sandwich was first made in Springfield in the 1920s. It is a hot, open-faced sandwich. Thick toast is topped with ham or hamburger. Then fries and cheese sauce are added.

The 1930s brought the Chicago-style hot dog. A beef hot dog is placed in a poppy-seed bun. It is then topped with mustard, relish, onion, tomato, pickled peppers, celery salt, and a pickle spear.

Sports are a big part of Illinois culture. The state has eight major professional sports teams. They all play in Chicago. The Cubs and White Sox are both baseball teams in the city.

Chicago-Style Pizza

Deep-dish pizza is a popular food in Chicago. It is also known as Chicago-style pizza. The pizza is cooked in a round pan with high edges. When people make Chicago-style pizza, they add cheese first and then tomato sauce.

Many college sports fans in Illinois enjoy cheering for teams from the University of Illinois Urbana-Champaign, *right*.

Soybeans are used to make food products such as tofu and soy milk.

Those who like hockey cheer for the Blackhawks. Basketball fans watch the Bulls and Sky play.

Industry

Many people in Illinois work in the energy industry. This includes jobs working with coal, oil, and nuclear energy. Illinois produces more electricity from nuclear energy than any other state.

Agriculture is another top industry in Illinois. Many farmers raise cattle, sheep, and **poultry**. The state is a leader in soybean and corn crops. Farmers also grow grains such as oats and buckwheat. Many fruits and vegetables are farmed in the state as well. Illinois grows more pumpkins than any other state.

Explore Online

Visit the website below. Does it give any new information about the Illiniwek nations that wasn't in Chapter Two?

Illinois

abdocorelibrary.com/discovering-illinois

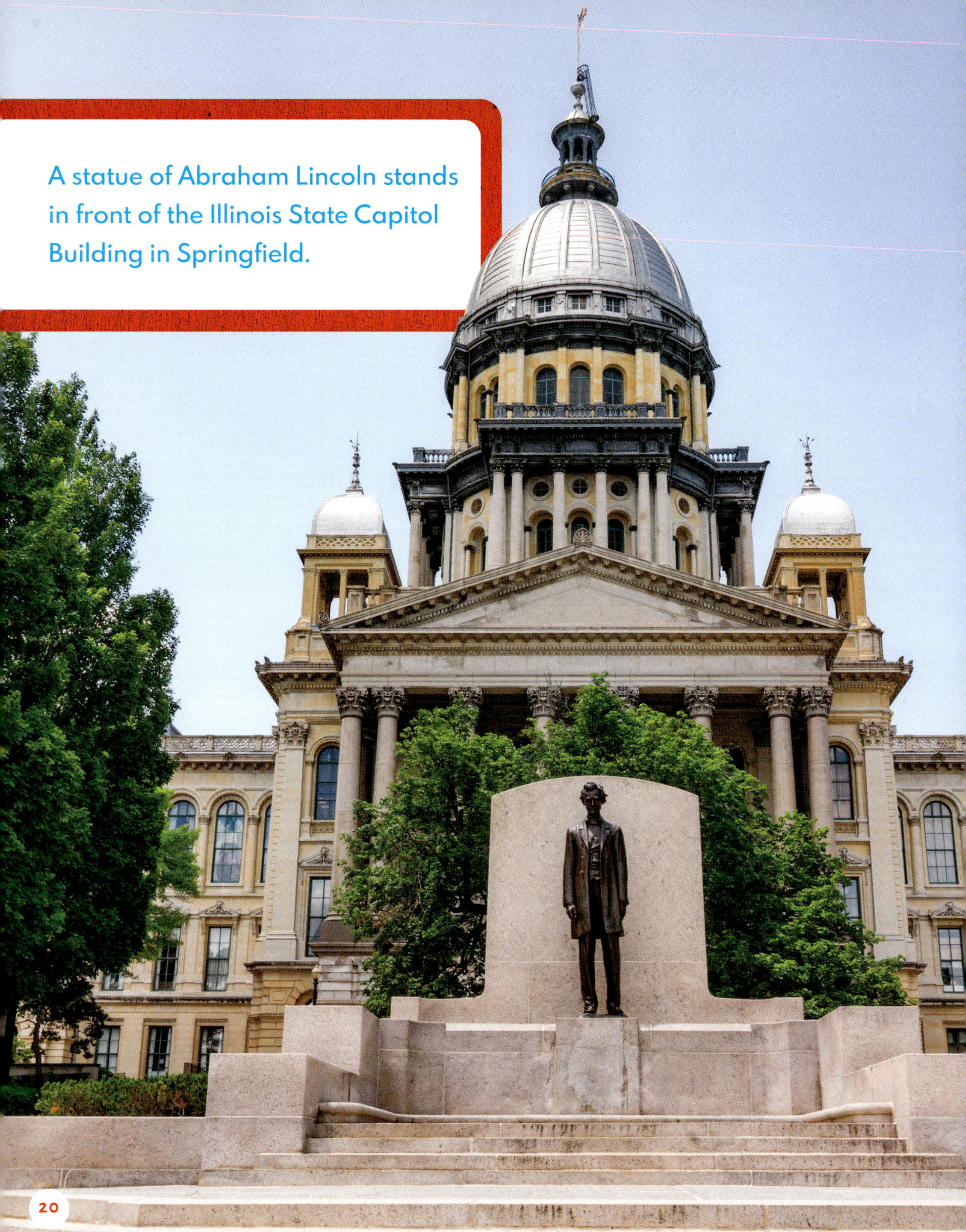
A statue of Abraham Lincoln stands in front of the Illinois State Capitol Building in Springfield.

Places in Illinois

Springfield is the capital of Illinois. President Abraham Lincoln lived there between 1837 and 1861. He left after he was elected president. Illinois is often called the Land of Lincoln.

Chicago is one of the most famous cities in the United States.

There are many things to do in Chicago. People can visit Millennium Park or Navy Pier. The Shedd Aquarium is also a popular attraction. Some other cities in Illinois include Champaign, Peoria, and Naperville.

Parks and Landmarks

Illinois has several state parks. Starved Rock State Park is a popular place to visit. It's located in Oglesby. Many American Indian nations used to live in the area. This included several Illiniwek nations. Today, visitors can hike through the park. They can also enjoy sights such as canyons, bluffs, trails, and waterfalls.

Cahokia Mounds State Historic Site is a notable Illinois landmark. It is in Collinsville.

Starved Rock State Park has 18 canyons, including the French, Wildcat, and Saint Louis.

The land holds the remains of an ancient American Indian **civilization**. In the 1000s CE, the city held as many as 20,000 people.

The city also had about 120 mounds of earth. People were buried under some of these mounds. Buildings stood on others.

There are several places in Springfield that honor Abraham Lincoln. The Lincoln Home is a national historic site. Lincoln lived there until he left the city. The Abraham Lincoln Presidential Library and Museum showcases Lincoln's life

Willis Tower

The Illinois landscape is flat. But its buildings are very tall. Chicago's Willis Tower is a famous skyscraper in the city. It was built in 1973 and was originally called the Sears Tower. Willis Tower stands at 1,450 feet (440 m) tall. It is the third-tallest building in North America.

Wrigley Field was originally called Weeghman Park. The field was renamed in 1926 to honor the Cubs' former owner, William Wrigley Jr.

and legacy. People can see the Lincoln Tomb at Oak Ridge Cemetery.

Chicago has several historic sports stadiums. Wrigley Field baseball stadium was built in 1914. It is home to the Cubs. Soldier Field has been a Chicago landmark since 1924. The Chicago Bears football team and Chicago Fire soccer team share the stadium.

Cloud Gate, also known as The Bean, is a popular tourist attraction in Chicago's Millennium Park.

There are many things to experience in Illinois. Visitors can try the many foods the state is famous for. Illinois has places to visit for those who enjoy sports or history. And people can explore the big cities and all they have to offer.

Abraham Lincoln left Springfield in 1861. Before leaving, he gave his Farewell Address, talking about his love for the city:

> To this place . . . I owe everything. Here I have lived a quarter of a century, and have passed from a young to an old man. . . . I now leave, not knowing when, or whether ever, I may return.

Source: "Farewell Address." *National Park Service*, n.d., home.nps.gov. Accessed 2 Dec. 2023.

What's the Big Idea?

Read this quote carefully. What is its main idea? Explain how the main idea is supported by details.

State Map

KEY

Capital

Park

City or town

Point of interest

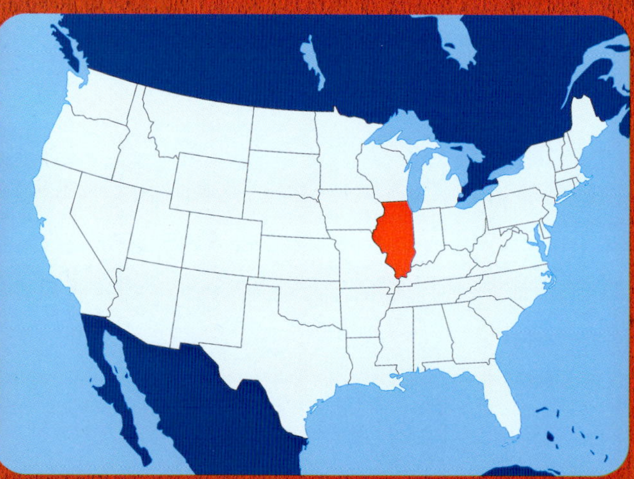

Starved Rock State Park

Lincoln Home National Historic Site

Chicago

Illinois: The Prairie State
Wisconsin
Lake Michigan
Wrigley Field
Iowa
Chicago
Starved Rock
State Park
Indiana
Peoria
University of Illinois
Urbana-Champaign
Illinois River
Springfield
Mississippi River
Lincoln Home
National Historic Site
Cahokia Mounds
State Historic Site
Missouri
Cave-In-Rock
State Park
N
W
E
S
Carbondale
Kentucky

Glossary

automatic
something that works by itself with little to no human control

civilization
an advanced society

descendants
people who are related to a person or group that lived in the past

humid
describing air that has a lot of moisture

iconic
something well known and widely recognized

poultry
birds, such as chickens and turkeys, raised for food

settlers
people who moved to a new area

Online Resources

To learn more about Illinois, visit our free resource websites below.

Visit **abdocorelibrary.com** or scan this QR code for free Common Core resources for teachers and students, including vetted activities, multimedia, and booklinks, for deeper subject comprehension.

Visit **abdobooklinks.com** or scan this QR code for free additional online weblinks for further learning. These links are routinely monitored and updated to provide the most current information available.

Learn More

Kavon, Kana. *The 50 States: Amazing Landscapes, Fascinating People, Wonderful Wildlife*. DK, 2021.

Kortemeier, Todd. *Chicago Bulls*. Abdo, 2023.

Murray, Julie. *Illinois*. Abdo, 2020.

Index

About the Author

Former longtime executive editor of *Girls' Life* magazine, Kelly Anne White is the award-winning author of *The Legend of the Fairy Stones*, *The Bible Adventure Book of Scavenger Hunts*, and other books for kids. Kelly has edited hundreds of books across genres for HarperCollins, Rockridge Press, Kirkus Editorial, and more. Currently, she serves as an editor for Scribe Media, indexer for Guideposts Books, and instructor for The PEN Institute.